SNUGGLY VIBES
COZY DREAMS
COLORING BOOK

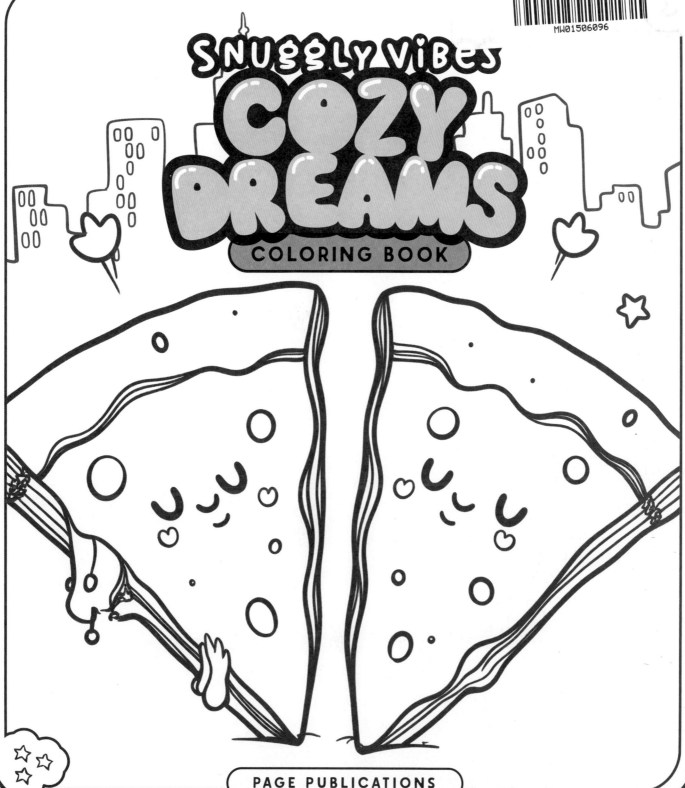

PAGE PUBLICATIONS

HiBERNATION♥N
STATI♥N

PURRFECTLY HAPPY

eggcellent
nap

pancakes
& pals

beach
break

pancakes
and unicorns

nestled in

peaceful
picnic

COZY
& CUTE

BEAR
WITH US

MagiCAL
DREAMS

FUZZY
FeLINeS

SNUG
IN A MUG

CHEERY
CHERRIES

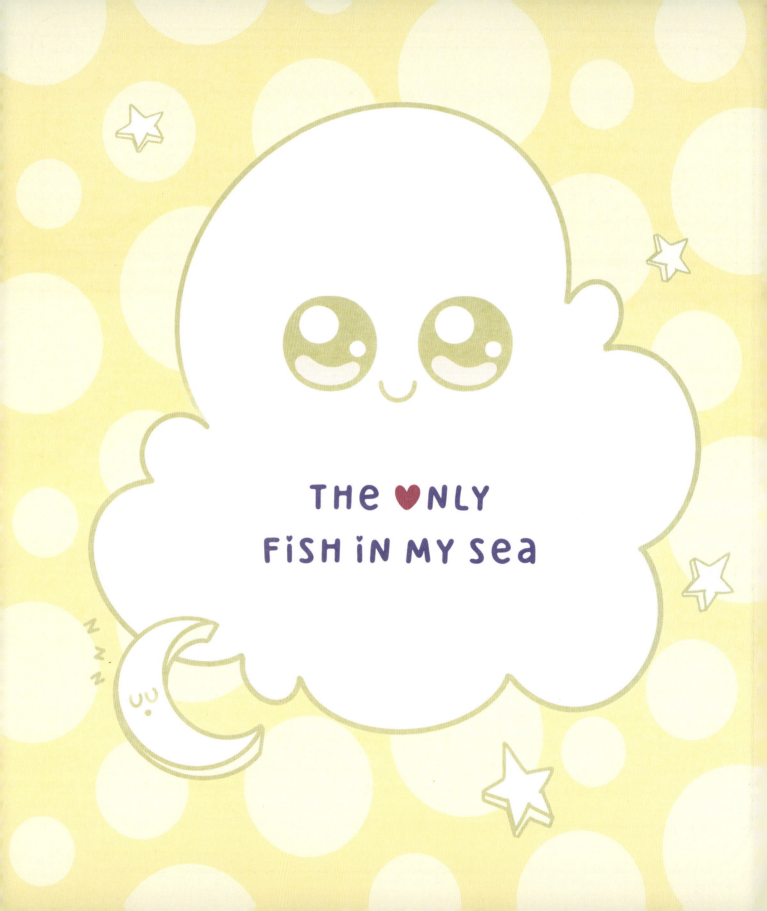

NIGHT
SKY

BUNDLED
UP

parked
in the dark

sleepy
at sea

ISBN: 978-1-64833-925-7